Wildebeests

By Mary Molly Shea

Gareth Stevens
Publishing

Please visit our Web site, www.garethstevens.com. For a free color catalog of all our high-quality books, call toll free 1-800-542-2595 or fax 1-877-542-2596.

Library of Congress Cataloging-in-Publication Data

Shea, Mary Molly.
 Wildebeests / Mary Molly Shea.
     p. cm. – (Animals that live in the grasslands)
 Includes index.
 ISBN 978-1-4339-3885-6 (pbk.)
 ISBN 978-1-4339-3886-3 (6-pack)
 ISBN 978-1-4339-3884-9 (library binding)
1. Gnus–Juvenile literature. 2. Grassland animals–Juvenile literature. I. Title.
 QL737.U53S476 2011
 599.64′59–dc22
                                        2010000407

First Edition

Published in 2011 by
Gareth Stevens Publishing
111 East 14th Street, Suite 349
New York, NY 10003

Designer: Michael J. Flynn
Editor: Therese Shea

Photo credits: Cover, pp. 1, 5, 7, 9, 11, 13, 15, 21, back cover Shutterstock.com; p. 17 Pedro Ugarte/AFP/Getty Images; p. 19 Andy Rouse/Riser/Getty Images.

Printed in the United States of America

CPSIA compliance information: Batch #CS10GS: For further information contact Gareth Stevens, New York, New York at 1-800-542-2595.

Table of Contents

Boldface words appear in the glossary.

A Wild Beast?

"Wildebeest" (WIHL-duh-beest) means "wild beast." It is a scary name. However, wildebeests eat only plants. Another name for a wildebeest is a gnu (NOO or NYOO).

A Wild Body!

Wildebeests live on the plains and **grasslands** of Africa. They have a big head, short neck, large body, and thin legs. Their shoulders are higher than their back end.

high shoulders

thin legs

7

A wildebeest has a black, grey, or brown body. It has a black mane. It also has a **beard** and tail. This hair may be black or white. All wildebeests have **horns**.

mane

horns

beard

9

Kinds of Wildebeests

There are different kinds of wildebeests. The blue wildebeest has hair with a silver-blue shine. It weighs a lot. Black wildebeests are much smaller.

black wildebeest

blue wildebeest

Western white-bearded wildebeests are the smallest. However, there are huge numbers of them! More than 1 **million** western white-bearded wildebeests live in Africa today.

Always Hungry

Wildebeests are always ready to eat. They eat day and night. They travel in giant herds looking for food and water. Wildebeests have special teeth for tearing and eating grass.

When it is hot, rivers dry up and grass dies. Some wildebeests **migrate** north each year to find food and water. They may travel hundreds of miles.

Clever Calves

Wildebeests look for **mates** each year. Eight months later, wildebeest calves are born. They start to walk in just minutes! Calves stay with their mother for about a year.

calf

Calves must keep up with the herd in order to stay alive. Wildebeests have many enemies. Lions and cheetahs hunt wildebeests. If wildebeests stay safe, they can live to be 20 years old.

Fast Facts

Height	up to 5 feet (1.5 meters)
Length	up to 8 feet (2.4 meters); tail may be 3 feet (0.9 meter) more
Weight	up to 600 pounds (270 kilograms)
Diet	grass
Average life span	about 20 years in the wild

Glossary

beard: a growth of longer hair on an animal's chin

grasslands: land on which grass is the main kind of plant life

horn: a hard, often pointed growth on an animal's head

mate: one of a pair of animals that come together to make a baby

migrate: to move from one place to another

million: a thousand thousands, or 1,000,000

For More Information

Books

Jackson, Kay. *Explore the Grasslands.* Mankato, MN: Capstone Press, 2007.

Walden, Katherine. *Wildebeests.* New York, NY: Rosen Publishing, 2009.

Web Sites

African Wildlife Foundation: Wildebeest
www.awf.org/content/wildlife/detail/wildebeest
Read many different facts about wildebeests, including how many are left in the world.

National Geographic: Wildebeest
animals.nationalgeographic.com/animals/mammals/wildebeest.html
Read more about wildebeests and listen to sounds they make.

Index

About the Author

Mary Molly Shea, a practicing nurse and forensic scientist, spends her free time rescuing animals in western New York and doing research for books like this one.